Corni
Cream Teas

– a guide to THE BEST

For further information of all the titles in this series please visit:-
www.tormark.co.uk

Designed by Alix Wood, www.alixwood.co.uk

Published by Tor Mark, United Downs Ind Est, Redruth,
Cornwall TR16 5HY

First published 2015

ISBN 978 085025 435 8

Printed by Booths Print, The Praze, Penryn, Cornwall TR10 8AA

As you may know there are many, many cafes and tea rooms in Cornwall, so this book is not intended to show every place you could enjoy a Cornish cream tea. It is to show you a good tea room in any part of Cornwall you may choose to visit.

I have used TripAdvisor as a partial guide, because if the public give a four or five star rating you can be fairly sure you are not going to be disappointed.
I have also visited and checked every one with my husband, it's a hard life, but hey someone has to do it!

We may have missed some really good ones, so I am adding an E-mail address so you can contact me if you find a better Cornish cream tea and, as the book will be regularly edited, we may include your choice. In addition I would be grateful to receive any changes in the details of any existing entries.

Thanks for reading my book and happy munching.

E-Mail: jenniehj2@gmail.com

Disabled: Restricted means access possible but very difficult. If a disabled toilet is not mentioned there isn't one.

Satnav: As you know post codes can refer to more than one building, but the one you require will be close by.

① RECTORY FARM TEA ROOMS

This ancient farmhouse, dating back to 1296, still has oak beams salvaged from ship wrecks along this coast. A top award winning tea room started 60 years ago by owner Jill's mother-in-law and her scone recipe is still used today. You might also like to visit the little gift shop.

Crosstown, Morwenstow, nr Bude
EX23 9SR

Tel. 01288 331251

Opening Times 11-5
Season Apr 2nd –Nov 2nd
Parking On site
Toilet Yes
Seating Outside Yes
Freshly Baked Scones Yes
Food Hygiene Rating 5
Cash, Cards Both Both
Dog Friendly Yes
Disabled Access Access & toilet

② MARGARET'S RUSTIC TEA GARDEN

One of Bude's hidden secrets, near to the beach nestled in a tiny valley, with a brook and quaint little bridge is Margaret's caravan cafe. The tea garden has been here since the 1960's when it was run by her mother. Not to be missed.

Northcott Mouth, Dunsmouth nr Bude
EX23 9EG

Tel. 01288 355 241

Opening Times 9.30-6
Season Apr to Oct
Parking On site
Toilet Yes
Seating Outside Yes
Freshly Baked Scones Yes
Food Hygiene Rating 4
Cash, Cards Both Cash only
Dog Friendly Yes
Disabled Access Poor but possible

3 THE CABIN

Right across the road from the beach and with fabulous views. Bright cheerful cafe with friendly helpful staff. You can come straight off the beach in sandy swimwear and sample one of their excellent cream teas.

Main St.
Crackington Haven
EX23 0JG

Tel. 01840 230238

Opening Times **9-late afternoon**
Season **All year**
Parking **Public**
Toilet **Yes**
Seating Outside **Yes**
Freshly Baked Scones **Yes**
Food Hygiene Rating **4**
Cash, Cards Both **Both**
Dog Friendly **Yes**
Disabled Access **Access, no toilet**

4 BOSCASTLE FARM CAFE

Contemporary, but traditional cafe, high up in the hills with fabulous sea views. Only 50 yds from the Coastal Path it seems a good place to stop for a cream tea and, with a certificate of excellence, who wouldn't.

Penally Hill, Hillsborough Farm, Boscastle.
PL35 0HH

Tel. 01840 250827

Opening Times **9-5**
Season **All year**
Parking **On site**
Toilet **Yes**
Seating Outside **Yes**
Freshly Baked Scones **Yes**
Food Hygiene Rating **5**
Cash, Cards Both **Both**
Dog Friendly **Outside**
Disabled Access **Access & toilet**

5 HARBOUR LIGHTS GARDEN

A small pretty garden in front of a very attractive building with room inside if you prefer. Friendly staff. Hard to imagine the devastation caused by the floods of 2004, when you sit here enjoying a superb cream tea.

Quayside
Boscastle
PL35 0HD

Tel. 01840 250953

Opening Times 10-5
Season Mar-Nov
Parking In village, public
Toilet Yes
Seating Outside Yes
Freshly Baked Scones Yes
Food Hygiene Rating 5
Cash, Cards Both Both
Dog Friendly Yes
Disabled Access Access, no toilet

6 KING ARTHUR'S CAFE

A very popular cafe in the in the heart of Tintagel, with great food and very good cheerful service. A Cream Tea would go down a treat, before you explore the castle or take a cliff walk.

Atlantic Rd
Tintagel
PL34 0DD

Tel. 07791900661

Opening Times 9-5
Season Feb-Nov
Parking Public
Toilet Yes
Seating Outside Yes
Freshly Baked Scones Yes
Food Hygiene Rating 5
Cash, Cards Both Both
Dog Friendly Yes
Disabled Access Access, no toilet

⑦ PENGENNA TEA GARDENS

Don't miss this tea garden tucked in just off main road. Really good service from the well trained teenagers. Really good cream tea using a recipe well guarded by the owners, mouth watering and the tea is good too.

Atlantic Road
Tintagel
PL34 0DD

Tel. 01840 770223

Opening Times 9.30-6.30
Season All year
Parking Castle car park
Toilet Public
Seating Outside Yes
Freshly Baked Scones Yes
Food Hygiene Rating 5
Cash, Cards Both Both
Dog Friendly Outside
Disabled Access Access & toilet

⑧ HILL TOP FARM SHOP AND CAFE

Rustic and with lovely rural views, you could sit inside or under the covered outside seating area near the farm shop and enjoy a very nice cream tea.

Slaughterbridge
Camelford
PL32 9TT

Tel. 01840 211518

Opening Times 9-6, 9-4 Sun
Season All year
Parking On site
Toilet Yes
Seating Outside Yes
Freshly Baked Scones Yes
Food Hygiene Rating 4
Cash, Cards Both Cash only
Dog Friendly Yes
Disabled Access Access, no toilet

9 CUP CAKES CAFE

A tiny stone cottage, possibly originally a fisherman's home, houses a tea room with a little courtyard. A lovely place to enjoy a cream tea whilst exploring Port Isaac (Home to the "Doc Martin" TV series)

Middle St.
Port Isaac
PL29 3RH

Tel. 01208 880523

Opening Times 9.30-4.30
Season New Year - Oct 31st
Parking Public
Toilet Yes
Seating Outside Courtyard
Freshly Baked Scones Yes
Food Hygiene Rating 5
Cash, Cards Both Both
Dog Friendly Outside
Disabled Access Access, no toilet

10 MOWHAY CAFE

On a beautiful sunny day, sit out in this lovely tree filled garden and when the weather is not so good the inside is lovely too. The children's Wendy House and toys make this a great place to enjoy a cream tea with all the family.

Skippers Close
Trebetherick, Polzeath
PL27 6SE

Tel. 01208 863660

Opening Times 10.30-4
Season Easter-Nov
Parking On site
Toilet Yes
Seating Outside Yes
Freshly Baked Scones Yes
Food Hygiene Rating 5
Cash, Cards Both Both
Dog Friendly Outside
Disabled Access Access & toilet

⑪ LELLIZZICK CREAM TEA GARDEN

A farm garden with very fine views of the rolling countryside above Hawkers Cove, nr Padstow. A child and dog friendly garden and a very good Cream Tea, just the job after a long walk.

Harbour Cove
Padstow
PL28 8HR

Tel. 01841 532838

Opening Times 12.30-5
Season Easter-Sept 30th
Parking On site
Toilet Yes
Seating Outside Yes
Freshly Baked Scones Yes
Food Hygiene Rating 4
Cash, Cards Both Both
Dog Friendly Yes
Disabled Access Access, no toilet

⑫ CHERRY TREE COFFEE HOUSE

Take a stroll through Padstow to this retro coffee house, situated right on the harbour. With its pastel china and seaside paintings, a pleasant place to enjoy a cream tea. Check out the cake portions for next time, big enough to share.

West Quay
Padstow
PL28 8AQ

Tel. 01841 532934

Opening Times 9-5
Season All year
Parking Public
Toilet Yes
Seating Outside No
Freshly Baked Scones Yes
Food Hygiene Rating 5
Cash, Cards Both Both
Dog Friendly No
Disabled Access Difficult access, no toilet

13 MANNA
TEA ROOM

If you wanted a blueprint for a tea room this would be it, absolutely perfect in every way. Great service and immaculate decor, managing to look modern and fresh and old fashioned at the same time. Have a cream tea here, you won't be disappointed.

The Platt
Wadebridge
PL27 7AE

Tel. 01208 816721

Opening Times 9.30-5.30
Season All year
Parking Public, behind shop
Toilet Yes
Seating Outside Yes
Freshly Baked Scones Yes
Food Hygiene Rating 5
Cash, Cards Both Cash only
Dog Friendly Yes
Disabled Access Access, no toilet

14 FOLLY
TEA ROOMS

The very attractive exterior invites you into a rustic old world interior, in the centre of busy Bodmin. Having a cream tea either in our out would be a very pleasant experience.

3 Turf St.
Mount Folly, Bodmin
PL31 2DH

Tel. 01208 269250

Opening Times 8.30-3.30 Mon-Sat
Season All year
Parking Public 100yds
Toilet Yes
Seating Outside Yes
Freshly Baked Scones Yes
Food Hygiene Rating 3
Cash, Cards Both Cash only
Dog Friendly In garden
Disabled Access Access, no toilet

⑮ BERRYFIELDS FARM TEA ROOMS

A very attractive tea garden, with great service. Lovely big heart shaped scones smothered in strawberries. You'll think you are in cream tea heaven!

Market Garden
Porthcothan
PL28 8PW

Tel. 01841 520178

Opening Times 10-6
Season All year Closed Wed
Parking On site
Toilet Yes
Seating Outside Yes
Freshly Baked Scones Yes
Food Hygiene Rating 5
Cash, Cards Both Both
Dog Friendly Yes
Disabled Access Access & toilet

⑯ CARNEWAS TEA ROOMS

A rustic tea room, overlooking the coast run by brothers Craig and Scott and their mother, who has run it for 30 years using a scone recipe that Waitrose offered an undisclosed sum for. Come along and have a great cream tea here.

Bedruthan Steps
St Eval, Newquay
PL27 7UW

Tel. 01637 860701

Opening Times 10.30-5
Season All year
Parking NT
Toilet Yes
Seating Outside Yes
Freshly Baked Scones Yes
Food Hygiene Rating 5
Cash, Cards Both Both
Dog Friendly Yes
Disabled Access Access & toilet

17 ST MAWGAN TEA ROOMS

An absolutely beautiful tea garden with flowers, grape vines and wisteria everywhere, although you would need to come midsummer to see that. A peaceful relaxing place to enjoy a fabulous cream tea.

St Mawgan in Pydar
Newquay
TR8 4EP

Tel. 01637 860303

Opening Times **9-5 or 6**
Season **All year**
Parking **On site**
Toilet **Yes**
Seating Outside **Yes**
Freshly Baked Scones **Yes**
Food Hygiene Rating **5**
Cash, Cards Both **Both**
Dog Friendly **Outside**
Disabled Access **Access, no toilet**

18 GOSS MOOR TEA GARDEN

A lovely terrace and garden to relax in, excellent friendly staff. A family run tea garden, both dog and children friendly. Kevin's years of catering experience shine through and you couldn't get a better cream tea if you tried.

Elmlee Moorlands Rd
St Columb
TR9 6HW

Tel. 01726 861113

Opening Times **10-4**
Season **Easter-Sept 30th**
Parking **On road**
Toilet **Yes**
Seating Outside **Yes**
Freshly Baked Scones **Yes**
Food Hygiene Rating **4**
Cash, Cards Both **Both**
Dog Friendly **Yes**
Disabled Access **Access, no toilet**

19 MARTHA'S TEA ROOM

Walking by you could not miss the fact this is a tea room, it is so much everyone's idea of how a tea room should look. Go in and meet Melanie Rose who named the place after her Nan Martha. Opened in March 2013 it's just the place to enjoy your cream tea.

2 Central Sq.
Newquay
TR7 1EX

Tel. 01637 498166

Opening Times 10-5.30 summer
Season All year
Parking Public harbour 50yds
Toilet Yes
Seating Outside Yes
Freshly Baked Scones Yes
Food Hygiene Rating 4
Cash, Cards Both Both
Dog Friendly Outside
Disabled Access Access, no toilet

20 HARBOUR REST CAFE

This little cafe taken over by Tracey and her partner 5 years ago, has a lovely warm atmosphere. Don't be put off by the outside, this is a work in progress. Great jam made by Tracey to go on your cream tea.

2 Southquay Hill
Newquay
TR7 1HR

Tel. 01637 850710

Opening Times 8-10
Season Summer and ½ terms
Parking Public harbour car park
Toilet Yes
Seating Outside No
Freshly Baked Scones Yes
Food Hygiene Rating 5
Cash, Cards Both Cash Only
Dog Friendly Yes
Disabled Access Access, no toilet

㉑ CAFE CLOUD

A delightful cafe right on the main street, near the harbour. Light and bright with great service and a really good cream tea. A good place to stop on the way home from the beach.

54 Fore Street.
Newquay
TR7 1LW

Tel. 07759968345

Opening Times **9.30-6.30**
Season **Feb-Nov**
Parking **Public, right behind**
Toilet **No**
Seating Outside **Yes**
Freshly Baked Scones **Yes**
Food Hygiene Rating **5**
Cash, Cards Both **Cash only**
Dog Friendly **Yes**
Disabled Access **Access, no toilet**

㉒ STEPPING STONES

Fresh modern interior, a friendly welcome and great service, just what you need after a day on the beach. A fresh cream tea will make your day perfect.

Boscawen Rd
Perranporth
TR6 0EW

Tel. 01872 573029

Opening Times **9-8**
Season **All year**
Parking **Public town car parks**
Toilet **Yes**
Seating Outside **Yes**
Freshly Baked Scones **Yes**
Food Hygiene Rating **4**
Cash, Cards Both **Both**
Dog Friendly **Yes**
Disabled Access **Access, no toilet**

23 WENDY'S COFFEE BARN

Set in a courtyard surrounded by little gift shops, great for Christmas and birthday gifts. What could be nicer than a cream tea and a bit of shopping.

Morgans Presingoll Barns
St Agnes
TR5 0PA

Tel. 01872 553007

Opening Times 10-5.30
Season All year
Parking On site
Toilet Yes
Seating Outside Yes
Freshly Baked Scones Yes
Food Hygiene Rating 5
Cash, Cards Both Both
Dog Friendly Yes
Disabled Access Access & toilet

24 OLIVE'S GARDEN

What a lovely setting for a tea garden with friendly staff and a fabulous cream tea. At night it's a simple bistro in this lovely old cottage. Jonny and Penny used to have Olive's in St Ives, another success story.

Hill Top Cottage
Porthtowan
TR4 8TY

Tel. 07546485061

Opening Times 10-10
Season Easter- Sept
Parking On site
Toilet Yes
Seating Outside Yes & inside
Freshly Baked Scones Yes
Food Hygiene Rating 5
Cash, Cards Both Cash only
Dog Friendly Yes
Disabled Access Access, no toilet

25 THE LILY TEA ROOMS

A lovely hidden treasure of a place, down a lane near Truro. While eating your cream tea on the raised decking, you can gaze out over a few of the 60 lily ponds.

Penrose Water Gardens
Shortlanesend nr Truro
TR4 9ES

Tel. 01872 222307

Opening Times 8.30-4.30 Sun 10-4
Season All year
Parking On site
Toilet Yes
Seating Outside Yes
Freshly Baked Scones Yes
Food Hygiene Rating 4
Cash, Cards Both Both
Dog Friendly Outside on leads
Disabled Access Access, no toilet

26 CHARLOTTE'S TEA HOUSE

You approach by wandering up the stairs, past fascinating antiques from the shop below. In a quaint old world setting you are greeted by a waitress dressed in Victorian costume. Try for a window seat with views of Truro's cobbled streets.

Coinage Hall
1 Boscawen St, Truro
TR1 1QU

Tel. 01872 263706

Opening Times 9.30-4.30
Season All year
Parking Public city parking
Toilet Yes
Seating Outside No
Freshly Baked Scones Yes
Food Hygiene Rating 5
Cash, Cards Both Both
Dog Friendly No
Disabled Access No access - upstairs

27 THE BAKING BIRD

Light modern and airy just behind the Cathedral. Not only a great place to get a good cream tea, but you can enjoy it in the colourful lounge upstairs. Check out the cup cakes too.

2 Old Bridge St.
Truro
TR 1 2AQ

Tel. 01872 277849

Opening Times 10-5 closed Sun
Season All year
Parking Public, opposite
Toilet Yes
Seating Outside No
Freshly Baked Scones Yes
Food Hygiene Rating 4
Cash, Cards Both Both
Dog Friendly No
Disabled Access Restricted, no toilet

28 THE CLOISTERS

Tucked away down an alley, a stone's throw from Truro Cathedral. Just the place to while away an hour savouring a delicious cream tea and retreating from the hustle and bustle of Truro.

Tippets Backlett
off River St, Truro
TR1 2TF

Tel. 01872 277774

Opening Times 9-4
Season All year
Parking Public city parking
Toilet Yes
Seating Outside No
Freshly Baked Scones Yes
Food Hygiene Rating 4
Cash, Cards Both Both
Dog Friendly No
Disabled Access Access & toilet

29 GRACEY'S TEA ROOM

A Grade 11 listed elegant Georgian House is the home of this popular family run tea room. Refurbished in 2014 and with a lovely south facing garden, you should definitely stop here for a top class cream tea.

Castle Lodge
10 Castle St, Truro
TR1 3AF

Tel. 01872 276690

Opening Times 8-5
Season All year
Parking Public city car parks
Toilet Yes
Seating Outside Yes
Freshly Baked Scones Yes
Food Hygiene Rating 5
Cash, Cards Both Both
Dog Friendly Outside
Disabled Access Restricted, no toilet

30 HALWYN TEA GARDEN

Beautiful tea garden with views down to the River Fal. One of my personal favourites, I know you will enjoy a cream tea here followed if you like by a wander through the woods down to the private beach.

Old Kea
Truro
TR3 6AW

Tel. 01872 272152

Opening Times 11-5
Season June-Aug 31st then weekends
Parking On site
Toilet Yes
Seating Outside Yes
Freshly Baked Scones Yes
Food Hygiene Rating 4
Cash, Cards Both Cash only
Dog Friendly Yes
Disabled Access Access, no toilet

③① PENVENTON PARK HOTEL

This is the place to go for a special C cream tea in a luxurious setting. A beautiful Georgian Mansion set in lovely wooded gardens and one of Cornwall's premier hotels, luckily this is not reflected in the price so treat yourself.

West End
Redruth
TR15 1TE

Tel. 01209 203000

Opening Times **All day**
Season **All year**
Parking **On site**
Toilet **Yes**
Seating Outside **Yes**
Freshly Baked Scones **Yes**
Food Hygiene Rating **5**
Cash, Cards Both **Both**
Dog Friendly **Outside/Lounge**
Disabled Access **Access & toilet**

③② HELL'S MOUTH CAFE

A cafe favoured by coastal walkers and visitors stopping to look at Hell's Mouth cliffs across the road. Stop in for a cream tea, it's always busy but that's a good sign.

Gwithian
Hayle
TR27 5EG

Tel. 01209 718419

Opening Times **9-5.30**
Season **Mar-Sept, weekends to Nov**
Parking **On site**
Toilet **Yes**
Seating Outside **Yes**
Freshly Baked Scones **Yes**
Food Hygiene Rating **5**
Cash, Cards Both **Both**
Dog Friendly **Yes**
Disabled Access **Access & toilet**

33 GODREVY BEACH CAFE

Set in Godrevy Beach NT car park and very handy for the long beautiful beaches of Gwithian Towans. Why not have a great cream tea here, after a walk on the beach.

Opening Times 10-5
Season All year
Parking NT car park
Toilet Yes
Seating Outside Yes
Freshly Baked Scones Yes
Food Hygiene Rating 5 Chefs Gold
Cash, Cards Both Both
Dog Friendly Downstairs
Disabled Access Access & toilet

Godrevy
Towans, Gwithian
TR27 5ED

Tel. 01736 757999

34 THE JAM POT

An unusual circular cafe was once a coastguard lookout post with views of St Ives Bay and Gwithian Towans. Famous locally for its quirky look and home cooked food. You couldn't fail to enjoy a cream tea here.

Opening Times 10-5
Season Easter-Sept
Parking Public, opp Surf Cafe
Toilet Yes
Seating Outside Yes
Freshly Baked Scones Yes
Food Hygiene Rating 5
Cash, Cards Both Cash only
Dog Friendly Yes
Disabled Access Difficult, no toilet

Gwithian Towans
nr Hayle
TR27 5BU

Tel. 01736 601114

35 MAD HATTER TEA ROOMS

A lovely snug little tea room overlooking the harbour in Hayle. A cream tea would be very welcome here served by the friendly welcoming staff.

73 Fore St.
Hayle
TR27 4DX

Tel. 01736 754241

Opening Times 10-4/5
Season Easter to Sept
Parking Public, across road
Toilet Yes
Seating Outside Yes
Freshly Baked Scones Yes
Food Hygiene Rating 5
Cash, Cards Both Both
Dog Friendly Yes
Disabled Access Access, no toilet

36 THE TEA ROOM

A very nice tea room with harbour views for people and boat watching on a sunny day. Beware the seagulls trying to enjoy your cream tea too.

1 Wharf House
The Wharf, St. Ives
TR26 1PG

Tel. 01736 794325

Opening Times 9.30-5
Season Feb- Dec
Parking Park and Ride
Toilet Yes
Seating Outside Yes
Freshly Baked Scones Yes
Food Hygiene Rating 5
Cash, Cards Both Both
Dog Friendly Yes
Disabled Access Access, no toilet

37 THE BEACHCOMBER

You can just pop off the beach for a lovely cream tea inside or out, just as nice. A visit to St Ives is not complete without one.

The Wharf
St Ives
TR26 1PU

Tel. 01736 794844

Opening Times **9-5.30**
Season **Easter-Oct 31st**
Parking **Park and Ride**
Toilet **Yes**
Seating Outside **Yes**
Freshly Baked Scones **Yes**
Food Hygiene Rating **4**
Cash, Cards Both **Both**
Dog Friendly **Yes**
Disabled Access **Access, no toilet**

---

38 OLIVES

A great cream tea, huge scone , lovely homemade jam and lashings of cream. Sandwiches are a work of art too. Lovely cafe just opposite the lane to Island Car Park.

Island Sq.
St Ives
TR26 1NX

Tel. 07759968345

Opening Times **10.30-5**
Season **Easter-Sept 31st**
Parking **Public, Island car park**
Toilet **Yes**
Seating Outside **Yes**
Freshly Baked Scones **Yes**
Food Hygiene Rating **5**
Cash, Cards Both **Cash Only**
Dog Friendly **Yes**
Disabled Access **Access outside, no toilet**

39 PORTHMEOR CAFE

Just across the road from Tate St Ives and with beautiful views of Porthmeor Beach. Perched on the sea wall, this attractive beach restaurant has a very good reputation, not least for its cream teas.

Porthmeor Beach
St Ives
TR26 1JZ

Tel. 01736 793366

Opening Times 9-9
Season   Easter-1st Nov
Parking Park and Ride
Toilet Yes
Seating Outside Yes
Freshly Baked Scones Yes
Food Hygiene Rating 5
Cash, Cards Both Both
Dog Friendly Outside
Disabled Access No Access

40 THE OLD CHAPEL CAFE

The Old Chapel is a guest house and a tea room, very popular with coastal walkers. A lovely comfy, airy tea room, so you can enjoy your cream tea there or take it outside and admire the lovely sea views, weather permitting.

Zennor
St Ives
TR26 3BY

Tel. 01736 798307

Opening Times 9-5
Season Easter-Oct 31st
Parking On site
Toilet Yes
Seating Outside Yes
Freshly Baked Scones Yes
Food Hygiene Rating 5
Cash, Cards Both Both
Dog Friendly Outside
Disabled Access Access outside, no toilet

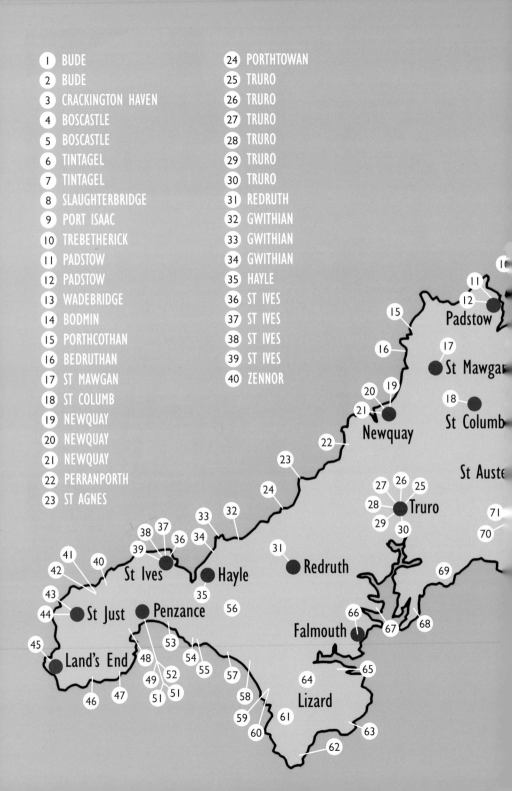

1 BUDE
2 BUDE
3 CRACKINGTON HAVEN
4 BOSCASTLE
5 BOSCASTLE
6 TINTAGEL
7 TINTAGEL
8 SLAUGHTERBRIDGE
9 PORT ISAAC
10 TREBETHERICK
11 PADSTOW
12 PADSTOW
13 WADEBRIDGE
14 BODMIN
15 PORTHCOTHAN
16 BEDRUTHAN
17 ST MAWGAN
18 ST COLUMB
19 NEWQUAY
20 NEWQUAY
21 NEWQUAY
22 PERRANPORTH
23 ST AGNES

24 PORTHTOWAN
25 TRURO
26 TRURO
27 TRURO
28 TRURO
29 TRURO
30 TRURO
31 REDRUTH
32 GWITHIAN
33 GWITHIAN
34 GWITHIAN
35 HAYLE
36 ST IVES
37 ST IVES
38 ST IVES
39 ST IVES
40 ZENNOR

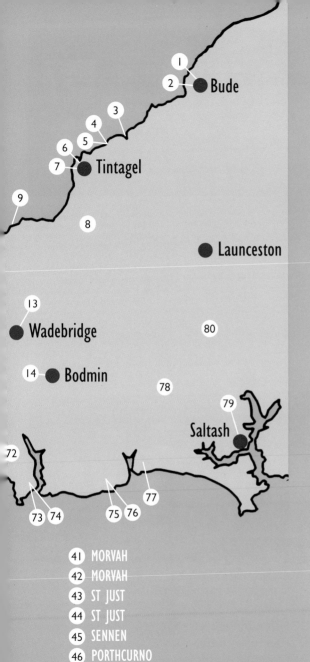

1   Bude
2

3
4
5
6
7   Tintagel
9
8   Launceston

13
Wadebridge
14   Bodmin
80
78
79   Saltash
72
73   74   75   76   77

49   PENZANCE
50   PENZANCE
51   PENZANCE
52   PENZANCE
53   ST MICHAEL'S MOUNT
54   PERRANUTHNOE
55   PERRANUTHNOE
56   LEEDSTOWN
57   PORTHLEVEN
58   HELSTON
59   POLDU
60   MULLION COVE
61   KYNANCE COVE
62   LIZARD POINT
63   COVERACK
64   CONSTANTINE
65   HELFORD
66   FALMOUTH
67   ST MAWES
68   PORTHSCATHO
69   VERYAN
70   MEVAGISSEY
71   MEVAGISSEY
72   CHARLESTOWN
73   FOWEY
74   FOWEY
75   POLPERRO
76   POLPERRO
77   EAST LOOE
78   LISKEARD
79   SALTASH
80   CALLINGTON

41   MORVAH
42   MORVAH
43   ST JUST
44   ST JUST
45   SENNEN
46   PORTHCURNO
47   MOUSEHOLE
48   TRENGWAINTON NT

41 LANYON TEA ROOM

Cream teas served on a working farm, nobody worries about wet dogs and muddy boots here. There's a paddock for your horse if you ride here. Large parties should phone ahead. Always a warm welcome.

Opening Times **2-5**
Season **Apr-Oct**
Parking **On road**
Toilet **Yes**
Seating Outside **Yes**

Lanyon Farm
Morvah Rd, Bonsullow
TR20 8NY

Freshly Baked Scones **Yes**
Food Hygiene Rating **4**
Cash, Cards Both **Cash/Cheques**
Dog Friendly **Yes**

Tel. 01736 351273

Disabled Access **Access, no toilet**

42 ROSEMERGY FARMHOUSE

A beautiful rural spot with a pretty farmhouse and gorgeous garden. Spectacular views. A perfect cream tea made for you by Jane, just adds to the perfection.

Opening Times **2-6**
Season **Apr-Oct 31st**
Parking **On site**
Toilet **Yes**
Seating Outside **Yes**

Morvah
Pendeen, nr Penzance
TR20 8YX

Freshly Baked Scones **Yes**
Food Hygiene Rating **5**
Cash, Cards Both **Cash only**
Dog Friendly **Outside**

Tel. 01736 796557

Disabled Access **Access & toilet**

43 TRENGWAINTON TEA ROOMS

Through an archway in the car park into a secret walled garden. A little suntrap where you can discover their great cream tea. Then perhaps a walk round the beautiful Trengwainton Gardens.

Opening Times   10-5 closed Fri Sat
Season   Mid Feb-Nov 2nd
Parking   On site
Toilet   Yes
Seating Outside   Yes
Madron
Penzance
TR20 8RZ

Freshly Baked Scones   Yes
Food Hygiene Rating   5 Platinum
Cash, Cards Both   Both
Dog Friendly   Outside
Tel. 01736 331717
Disabled Access   Access & toilet

44 KEGEN TEG

Good homemade organic food leaning towards veggie. Cheerful friendly cafe with a good atmosphere. While eating your cream tea check out the beautiful ceiling.

Opening Times   9-6
Season   All year
Parking   Public, in village
Toilet   Yes
Seating Outside   No
12 Market Street
St Just
TR19 7HD

Freshly Baked Scones   Yes
Food Hygiene Rating   5
Cash, Cards Both   Cash only
Dog Friendly   Yes
Tel. 01736 788562
Disabled Access   Access, no toilet

㊺ THE COOK BOOK CAFE

A unique book shop and cafe combined with newspapers and books to read whilst you enjoy your cream tea. Sure to be good in this Platinum award winning cafe.

Opening Times 10-5(summer) 10-4(winter)
Season All year
Parking Public, in village
Toilet In car park
Seating Outside Yes

4 Cape Cornwall St.
St. Just
TR19 7JZ

Freshly Baked Scones Yes
Food Hygiene Rating 5 Platinum
Cash, Cards Both Both
Dog Friendly Yes

Tel. 01736 787266

Disabled Access Access, no toilet

㊻ THE APPLE TREE CAFE

A pretty cafe in a lovely setting, on the road to Porthcurno. Set up by the local community as a place to meet each other, but don't worry all are welcome here for a cream tea or whatever else you want.

Opening Times 10-5
Season All year
Parking On site
Toilet Yes
Seating Outside Yes

Trevescan
Sennen
TR19 7AQ

Freshly Baked Scones Yes
Food Hygiene Rating 5 Gold Chef
Cash, Cards Both Both, cards min £10
Dog Friendly Yes

Tel. 01736 872753

Disabled Access No Access, steps

47 PORTHCURNO BEACH CAFE

A friendly seaside cafe a stone's throw from the beach and opposite the beach car park. After a day on the beach or a visit to the famous Minack outdoor theatre, enjoy a lovely cream tea here.

Opening Times **9-6**
Season **Easter-Sept 30th + ½ term**
Parking **Public, opposite**
Toilet **In car park**
Seating Outside **Yes**
Freshly Baked Scones **Yes**
Food Hygiene Rating **5**
Cash, Cards Both **Both**
Dog Friendly **Outside**
Disabled Access **Access, no toilet**

Porthcurno
St Levan
TR 19 6JX

Tel. 01736 810834

48 ROCK POOL CAFE

A bright sunny cafe, leaning towards shabby chic with lovely vintage china and a view to linger over. Before you go down to the rock pools below, find time for a sumptuous cream tea and maybe spot a dolphin or two.

Opening Times **10-6**
Season **All year weekends in winter**
Parking **Public, on site**
Toilet **Yes**
Seating Outside **Yes**
Freshly Baked Scones **Yes**
Food Hygiene Rating **5**
Cash, Cards Both **Both**
Dog Friendly **Yes**
Disabled Access **Access, no toilet**

The Parade
Mousehole
TR19 6PR

Tel. 01736 762000

49 ADELE'S TEA ROOMS

An old world tea rooms in one of the oldest buildings in Penzance and steeped in the history of the town. Have a seat, soak up the atmosphere and enjoy one of Adele's famous cream teas.

Opening Times **8-8**
Season **All year**
Parking **Public, nearby**
Toilet **Yes**
Seating Outside **Yes**

The Barbican,
Barbican Lane, Penzance
TR18 4EF

Freshly Baked Scones **Yes**
Food Hygiene Rating **5**
Cash, Cards Both **Cash only**
Dog Friendly **Yes**

Tel. 01736 366693

Disabled Access **No access, steep steps**

50 HARBOURSIDE CAFE

Recently refurbished, this smart little cafe sells freshly cooked meals with great portions and their cream teas are delicious. Hopefully you can sit outside in the sun and watch the boats go by.

Opening Times **7.30-6**
Season **All year**
Parking **Public, nearby**
Toilet **Yes**
Seating Outside **Yes**

Wharf Rd.
Penzance
TR18 4AA

Freshly Baked Scones **Yes**
Food Hygiene Rating **5**
Cash, Cards Both **Cash only**
Dog Friendly **Yes**

Tel. 01736 362405

Disabled Access **Access & toilet**

51 LOST AND FOUND CAFE

This hidden away cafe is shabby chic with a quirky twist, so tucked away it could easily be missed, but the effort will be worth it. After your cream tea you could have a browse round the vintage shop.

16 Chapel St.
Penzance
TR 18 4AW

Tel. 07792358110

Opening Times 9.30-5.30
Season   All year
Parking   Public, Green Market
Toilet Yes
Seating Outside Yes
Freshly Baked Scones   Yes
Food Hygiene Rating 5
Cash, Cards Both Both
Dog Friendly Yes
Disabled Access Access at back, no toilet

52 GREEN PIG FARM TEA ROOM

A log cabin set on a hill above amazing views of St. Michaels Mount and surrounding coast line. A pretty garden with plenty of seating. a little Cornish haven.

Ludgvan,
nr Penzance
TR20 8BG

Tel. 07976072871

Opening Times 11-5 closed Sat
Season   Easter- Sept 30th
Parking   On site
Toilet Yes
Seating Outside Yes
Freshly Baked Scones   Yes
Food Hygiene Rating 5
Cash, Cards Both Cash only
Dog Friendly Yes
Disabled Access Access, no toilet

53 ISLAND CAFE

This is a bit different, you either have to catch an island boat or walk over the causeway at low tide. Sit in the garden of this lovely local stone tea room and gaze out over the great sea views. A cream tea with a little adventure.

St. Michaels Mount,
Marazion
TR17 0HS

Tel. 01736 710507

Opening Times 9-5 Closed Sat
Season Mar-Nov
Parking Not needed
Toilet Yes
Seating Outside Yes
Freshly Baked Scones Yes
Food Hygiene Rating 5 Platinum
Cash, Cards Both Both
Dog Friendly Outside
Disabled Access Very restricted

54 PEPPERCORN KITCHEN

A very nice cafe, in the centre of the village. Enjoy an especially lovely cream tea, but don't forget to pop back another day for one of their amazing meringues or cakes.

CAFE, Lynfields Yard
Perranuthnoe, nr Penzance
TR20 9NE

Tel. 01736 719584

Opening Times 10-5
Season All year, closed Mon
Parking On site
Toilet Yes
Seating Outside Yes
Freshly Baked Scones Yes
Food Hygiene Rating 5
Cash, Cards Both Cash only
Dog Friendly Yes
Disabled Access Access & toilet

55 THE CABIN BEACH CAFE

Set above the beach in a little field is a lovely log cabin cafe with a large seating area with lovely views out over the sea. A cream tea here really hits the spot.

Perranuthnoe Beach
TR20 9NE

Tel. 01736 711733

Opening Times **8.30-7**
Season **All year winter 10-4**
Parking **Public, in village**
Toilet **In car park**
Seating Outside **Yes**
Freshly Baked Scones **Yes**
Food Hygiene Rating **5**
Cash, Cards Both **Both**
Dog Friendly **Yes**
Disabled Access **Access & toilet**

56 LITTLE PENGELLY FARM

An attractive house surrounded by little holiday cottages and a lovely mature garden and tea room. Nice friendly staff and a very fine cream tea. A light airy conservatory if the weathers not too good.

Trenwheal
Leedstown
TR27 6BP

Tel. 01736 850452

Opening Times **Check website**
Season **Apr-Sept**
Parking **On site**
Toilet **Yes**
Seating Outside **Yes**
Freshly Baked Scones **Yes**
Food Hygiene Rating **5**
Cash, Cards Both **Both**
Dog Friendly **Yes**
Disabled Access **Access, no toilet**

57 NAUTI BUT ICE

This tea room shares it space with a rather nice ice cream parlour. Sitting inside or out you can eat a cream tea here, whilst watching the comings and goings of a busy working fishing harbour.

Commercial Rd
Porthleven
TR13 9JE

Tel. 01326 573747

Opening Times 9-5
Season All year
Parking Public, by harbour
Toilet Yes
Seating Outside Yes
Freshly Baked Scones Yes
Food Hygiene Rating 5
Cash, Cards Both Both
Dog Friendly Yes
Disabled Access Difficult access, no toilet

58 HELSTON CUP AND CAKE

Lovely smart high street cafe in the heart of Helston, with amazing light scones, great coffee and tea. Lovely friendly staff giving everyone a warm welcome.

19 Menage St.
Helston
TR13 8AA

Tel. 07773001110

Opening Times 9-5 Mon-Sat
Season All year
Parking Public, 100yds
Toilet No
Seating Outside No
Freshly Baked Scones Yes
Food Hygiene Rating 5
Cash, Cards Both Cash only
Dog Friendly No
Disabled Access Difficult access, no toilet

59 POLPEOR CAFE

A view to take your breath away, the staff are always happy to point the seals out to you swimming in the cove below. Good friendly service and a super cream tea - you couldn't want more.

Opening Times 10-7 Sun11-4
Season Easter-Sept 31st
Parking Public, past lighthouse
Toilet Yes
Seating Outside Yes
Freshly Baked Scones Yes
Food Hygiene Rating 5
Cash, Cards Both Both
Dog Friendly Yes
Disabled Access Access to patio, no toilet

Lizard Peninsula
The Lizard
TR12 7NU

Tel. 01326 290898

60 POLDHU BEACH CAFE

Poldhu is definitely the place to have a cream tea, right on the beach with great views. You can enjoy one all year round with great service too. You can take your dog to the cafe, but not on the beach in the season.

Opening Times 9-6
Season 364 Days
Parking Public, across the road
Toilet Yes
Seating Outside Yes
Freshly Baked Scones Yes
Food Hygiene Rating 5
Cash, Cards Both Both
Dog Friendly Yes
Disabled Access Difficult access, no toilet

Poldhu Beach Cafe
Mullion
TR12 7JB

Tel. 01326 240530

61 MULLION COVE HOTEL

If you are in need of an idea for a special occasion, look no further. A cream tea on the terrace or in the lounge of this imposing hotel, feels really special. Overlooking Mullion harbour it is well worth a visit.

Opening Times Available all day
Season All year
Parking On site
Toilet Yes
Seating Outside Yes
Mullion Cove
Freshly Baked Scones Yes
The Lizard
Food Hygiene Rating 5
TR12 7EP
Cash, Cards Both Both
Dog Friendly Yes
Tel. 01326 240328
Disabled Access Access & toilet

62 KYNANCE BEACH CAFE

One of the most southerly points in Britain and designated an Area of Outstanding Natural Beauty. Cafe nestles on a hill above the beautiful Kynance Cove. Quite definitely a place to stop off for a cream tea.

Opening Times 10-5/7
Season Mar-Nov
Parking NT car park
Toilet Yes - no disabled
Seating Outside Yes
Kynance Beach
Freshly Baked Scones Yes
The Lizard
Food Hygiene Rating 5
TR12 7PJ
Cash, Cards Both Both
Dog Friendly No
Tel. 01326 290436
Disabled Access no toilet

63 HARBOUR LIGHTS

Placed on the seafront at Coverack, this is actually a bistro, but they serve amazing cream teas and how could they fail to be when the chef used to work for Jamie Oliver.

The Seafront
Coverack
TR12 6TE

Tel. 01326 280612

Opening Times 10-4
Season Feb-Dec
Parking Public village car park
Toilet Yes
Seating Outside Yes
Freshly Baked Scones Yes
Food Hygiene Rating 5
Cash, Cards Both Both
Dog Friendly Outside
Disabled Access Restricted, steps, no toilet

64 POTAGER GARDEN CAFE

An amazing renovated plant nursery with a beautiful double glazed green house as the tea room. a lovely wooded garden with swings and hammocks strung among the trees. Games galore and even a tightrope walk. It's a relaxing haven and just the place for a cream tea.

High Cross
Constantine, Falmouth
TR11 5RF

Tel. 01326 341258

Opening Times Fri Sat Sun 10-5
Season Mar-Dec
Parking On site, donation
Toilet Yes
Seating Outside Yes
Freshly Baked Scones Yes
Food Hygiene Rating 5
Cash, Cards Both Cash only
Dog Friendly On leads
Disabled Access Access & toilet

65 DOWN BY THE RIVERSIDE

A converted chapel maintaining many original features, in a delightful woodland setting overlooking the Helford River. They do a very fine cream tea, but are also well known for their crab sandwiches too. For Satnav ignore Treath turning.

Helford Chapel
The Lizard
TR12 6LB

Tel. 01326 231893

Opening Times 10-4/6
Season Easter-Oct 31st
Parking On site, public car park
Toilet Yes
Seating Outside Yes
Freshly Baked Scones Yes
Food Hygiene Rating 5
Cash, Cards Both Both
Dog Friendly Yes
Disabled Access Access, no toilet

66 DOLLY'S TEA ROOM

Probably the most beautiful room in Falmouth is home to Dolly's, a tea room by day and a wine bar by night with gin served in teapots, it's more of a speakeasy than a wine bar. Stay for a cream tea in the company of a pearl wearing Labrador.

21 Church Street
Falmouth
TR11 3EG

Tel. 01326 218400

Opening Times 10-10ish
Season All year
Parking Public, New Street
Toilet Yes
Seating Outside No
Freshly Baked Scones Yes
Food Hygiene Rating 4
Cash, Cards Both Both
Dog Friendly Well behaved
Disabled Access No access - upstairs

67 ST MAWES CAFE

New owners Sebastian and his wife are fulfilling a dream of opening a coffee shop in Cornwall. Situated in an arcade at the entrance to the main car park, this comfortable little cafe is well worth you popping in for a homemade cream tea.

Opening Times **8-6**
Season **All year**
Parking **On site, public car park**
Toilet **In car park**
Seating Outside **Yes**
Freshly Baked Scones **Yes**
Food Hygiene Rating **5**
Cash, Cards Both **Both**
Dog Friendly **Outside**
Disabled Access **Yes + Toilet in car park**

6 The Arcade
St Mawes
TR2 5DT

Tel. 01326 279173

---

68 TREGAIREWOON FARM KITCHEN

A bright, airy purpose built tea room on a working farm. A warm welcome awaits from Anne and her staff. You will come back again and again and not only for her great cream teas.

Open Times **MTWS 11.30-5.30: FSu 2.30-5.30**
Season **Easter-Sept 31st**
Parking **On site**
Toilet **Yes**
Seating Outside **Yes**
Freshly Baked Scones **Yes**
Food Hygiene Rating **5**
Cash, Cards Both **Cash Only**
Dog Friendly **Outside**
Disabled Access **Access & toilet**

Porthscatho
TR2 5EP

Tel. 07967826405

69 MELINSEY MILL

Set in pretty woodland 16th Century Melinsey Mill is the smallest working mill in Cornwall and would be a great day out without a cream tea, but with one its quite perfect.

Opening Times 10-5.30
Season Apr-Oct
Parking On site
Toilet Yes
Seating Outside Yes

Veryan
Roseland
TR2 5TX

Freshly Baked Scones Yes
Food Hygiene Rating 4
Cash, Cards Both Both
Dog Friendly Yes

Tel. 01872 501049

Disabled Access Access & toilet

70 TEA ON QUAY

Family owned tea room opened August 2014 and sits right on the edge of the quay, great for people and boat watching. Enjoy a homemade cream tea and maybe get some fresh fish on the way home.

Opening Times 10.30-5.00
Season All year
Parking Main car park
Toilet Yes + Disabled
Seating Outside No

West Wharf
Mevagissey
PL26 6UJ

Freshly Baked Scones Yes
Food Hygiene Rating 4
Cash, Cards Both Both
Dog Friendly Yes

Tel. 01726 844819

Disabled Access Yes

71 CHARLIE'S COFFEE HOUSE

Charlie's is a family run cafe in a converted post office, with squishy sofas and daily newspapers to read. A really chilled place to have a cream tea. Also Charlie's Boathouse near the harbour does great cream teas too and has disabled facilities. Open 10-9.

79 Charlestown Road
St Austell
PL25 3NJ

Tel. 01726 63322

Opening Times 9-4
Season All year
Parking On road
Toilet Yes
Seating Outside Yes
Freshly Baked Scones Yes
Food Hygiene Rating 5
Cash, Cards Both Both
Dog Friendly Outside
Disabled Access No Access

72 LOST GARDENS OF HELIGAN

Amazing gardens, farm shop and plant store. Definitely worth spending a day here, exploring and admiring all the work that went into this renovation. Then you can round off your day with a gorgeous cream tea.

Pentewan
St Austell
PL26 6EN

Tel. 01726 845100

Opening Times 9.30-5.30
Season All year
Parking On site
Toilet Yes
Seating Outside Yes
Freshly Baked Scones Yes
Food Hygiene Rating 5
Cash, Cards Both Both
Dog Friendly Outside
Disabled Access Access & toilet

73 THE DWELLING HOUSE

This beautiful elegant building in the High St dates back before Columbus discovered America and houses a traditional tea room. A truly unique place to share a cream tea, or you could try the cute little walled garden in good weather.

6 Fore St.
Fowey
PL23 2AQ

Tel. 01726 833662

Opening Times 10-6.30
Season All year except Jan
Parking Main public car park
Toilet Yes
Seating Outside Yes
Freshly Baked Scones Yes
Food Hygiene Rating Rating pending
Cash, Cards Both Cash or cheque
Dog Friendly Garden
Disabled Access No access

74 THE WELL HOUSE

A lovely beamed tea room with a wealth of stories and history dates back to 1430 and is the oldest house in Fowey. When eating a cream tea here, you feel as though you have been transported back to another time.

31-35 fore St.
Fowey
PL23 1AH

Tel. 01726 833832

Opening Times 10-5
Season Mid Jan-Mid Dec
Parking Main public car park
Toilet Yes
Seating Outside Yes
Freshly Baked Scones Yes
Food Hygiene Rating Rating pending
Cash, Cards Both Both
Dog Friendly Yes
Disabled Access Difficult access, no toilet

75 PLANTATION TEA ROOMS

If the weather permits, sit outside in the wonderful garden with its little stream wandering down to the harbour. Friendly staff are waiting to serve you a lovely cream tea.

The Coombes
Polperro
PL13 2RG

Tel. 01503 272223

Opening Times 10.30-5.30
Season 1st Mar-30th Sept
Parking Main public car park
Toilet Yes
Seating Outside Yes
Freshly Baked Scones Yes
Food Hygiene Rating 5
Cash, Cards Both Both
Dog Friendly Yes
Disabled Access Access, no toilet

76 MUSEUM TEA ROOMS

Wander down the little passageways to the harbour and you come across this rustic tea room by the water. Order a cream tea and you won't be bored with so much to see in the harbour.

The Warren
Polperro
PL13 2RB

Tel. 07772340056

Opening Times 9-3/6
Season Mar-Sept
Parking Main public car park
Toilet Yes
Seating Outside Yes
Freshly Baked Scones Yes
Food Hygiene Rating 5
Cash, Cards Both Cash only
Dog Friendly Yes
Disabled Access No access

⑦⑦ DAISY'S CAFE

A small cosy cafe just off the main street and just the place to pop into and enjoy a delightful cream tea. A welcome retreat from the busy street outside. Sadly no seating outside but a friendly atmosphere inside.

Opening Times 9-4.30
Season All year
Parking Public, by harbour
Toilet Yes
Seating Outside Yes

Castle Street
East Looe
PL13 1BA

Freshly Baked Scones Yes
Food Hygiene Rating 5
Cash, Cards Both Cash only
Dog Friendly Yes

Tel. 7988803315

Disabled Access Access, no toilet

⑦⑧ CAFE FLEUR

A lovely, bright, fun cafe with a lot of attention to detail. Caroline and her staff will happily tend to you and it's handily in the middle of a garden centre. You can wander around and then reward yourself with one of her wonderful cream teas.

Opening Times 9-4
Season All year
Parking On site
Toilet Yes
Seating Outside Yes

Goldenbank Garden Centre
Plymouth Rd Liskeard
PL14 3PB

Freshly Baked Scones Yes
Food Hygiene Rating 5
Cash, Cards Both Both
Dog Friendly Yes

Tel. 07565102889

Disabled Access Access & toilet

(79) THE BOOKSHELF TEA ROOM

A super bookshop, with a relaxing cafe upstairs and down. There is also a small balcony in good weather. An interesting place to stop and browse and enjoy a very good cream tea.

96 Fore St.
Saltash
PL12 6JW

Tel. 01752 845804

Opening Times 9-5 Sat 9-3
Season All year
Parking Public, 100 yds
Toilet Yes
Seating Outside Yes
Freshly Baked Scones Yes
Food Hygiene Rating 5
Cash, Cards Both Both
Dog Friendly Downstairs
Disabled Access Downstairs, no toilet

(80) ANNIE'S TEA ROOM

A lovely traditional cafe, in the heart of Callington popular with locals, always a good sign. A warm welcome awaits you, definitely the place in Callington to have a good cream tea.

11 Fore Street
Callington
PL17 7AA

Tel. 01579 383303

Opening Times 8.30-5.30
Season All year
Parking Public town car parks
Toilet Yes
Seating Outside Yes
Freshly Baked Scones Yes
Food Hygiene Rating 5
Cash, Cards Both Both
Dog Friendly Outside
Disabled Access Restricted, steps, no toilet